PATRIOTIC COLORING BOOK: AMERICA THE BEAUTIFUL

ARTHUR BENJAMIN

Maestro Publishing Group

Pubished by Maestro Publishing Group

Printed in the United States of America
ISBN: 978-1619495425

Get in touch with America's roots through this patriotic coloring book. From the Declaration of Independence to Washington Crossing the Delaware to the Wild West, get in touch with what made America great with these copies of America's most famous patriotic paintings. Great for adults and kids alike, this book is a must for any patriot.

CONTENTS

Plate 1
John Trumbull, *Declaration of Independence*, 1818 (placed 1826),
Rotunda, U. S. Capitol, Washington, D.C.

During his military service, John Trumbull created numerous historical paintings and portraits that stood as a particular testament to the American Revolution. In his mind, art should be useful to society, so he tried to preserve the memory of glorious events and eminent men and express his own political opinion and loyalty. In 1817, the U.S. Congress commissioned four large canvasses from Trumbull for the Rotunda of the Capitol at Washington, D.C. This one depicts the members of a committee that created a draft of the Declaration of Independence in the moment when they presented the draft to the Congress on June 28, 1776. He portrayed most of the individuals during life in the Neoclassical style. A reproduction of this painting is on the reverse side of the United States two-dollar bill.

Plate 2
Emanuel Leutze, *Washington Crossing the Delaware*, 1851,
Metropolitan Museum of Art, New York City

Leutze was born in Germany. Influenced by European academic art, especially German Romanticism, he remained close to the Düsseldorf school of painting. Elaborate composition, excellent drawing, and heroic motifs were constant elements of his style. This canvas is the second version he painted of the same subject. It depicts George Washington attacking the Hessians (German soldiers of British Empire) at Trenton, New Jersey, on December 25, 1776. His brave action and celebrated victory was a symbol of American patriotism. Leutze created an idealized scene with many incorrect details, but nevertheless, the painting was very popular during his time and widely reproduced in America and Germany.

Plate 3
Gilbert Stuart, *George Washington (Landsdowne portrait)*, 1796,
National Portrait Gallery, Smithsonian Institution, Washington, D.C.

This full-length portrait is an iconic, almost sacred, representation of George Washington, the father of the country. It was commissioned from the artist in 1796, the last year of Washington's presidency, as a gift to Marquis of Lansdowne, a British supporter of American independence. Stuart made several replicas of this picture, and more than one hundred portraits of George Washington. Because he studied painting in Europe, he included many symbolic details and the decorum of European royalty portraiture. The dignified leader is depicted in the classical orator's pose, wearing a formal, elegant black suit. The artist managed to capture the inner character of this important man and the impressive strength of his face. Decorative elements of the composition (books and pillars, landscape with rainbow, etc.) each have a complex, emblematic meaning.

Plate 4
John Singleton Copley, *Watson and the Shark*, 1778,
National Gallery of Art, Washington, D.C.

In 1749, a 14-year-old boy, Brook Watson, was swimming alone in Havana Harbor when a shark attacked him. Fishermen rescued him, but he lost his right foot. Later, he became a famous British politician and a successful trader. Copley chose this unique subject for his large painting and depicted the dramatic moment of Watson's sea battle with a horrible monster. Inspired by old masters of Renaissance and Baroque style,such as Rafael and Rubens, he achieved a dynamic structure and turbulent atmosphere. The emotional subject matter of the painting was very popular in his time, and he made many copies of it, as well as engravings based on it.

Plate 5
Albert Bierstadt, *The Rocky Mountains, Lander's Peak*, 1863,
Metropolitan Museum of Art, New York City

This is one of many panoramic views of the American frontier painted by Bierstadt. In 1859, he traveled for the first time to the West, where he spent time in the territories of Colorado and Wyoming as part of a government expedition. There, he made sketches and studies of everyday life and customs. Back in his studio in New York, he combined this interest in the factual with his interest in light and shadow, and created idyllic landscapes. He was influenced by the romantic style utilized in the Hudson River and Düsseldorf schools of painting. His audience admired this pastoral scene of an American Indian village. Theatrically arranged, with soft light and colors, it inspired the image of America as an exotic promised land. The beauty of nature became a source of great national pride.

Plate 6
Thomas Sully, *Passage of the Delaware*, 1819,
Museum of Fine Arts, Boston

Sully was a famous portraitist in his time; he rarely painted historical compositions. The state of North Carolina commissioned this painting for the Senate Hall in Raleigh, but his final product was too large for the space. The subject of this work was the wise and daring decision of General George Washington to cross the river. This was an important moment for the American Revolution: Washington was able to surprise the enemy and gain a crucial victory. Sully depicted this scene in a narrative, realistic style. He used clean, refined lines and contrast between light and dark to represent the commander's calmness and determination, and to intensify the significance of this historical campaign.

Plate 7
Frederic Remington, *Aiding a Comrade*, 1890,
Museum of Fine Arts, Houston

Frederic Remington, a well-known illustrator of the old American West, traveled frequently to Kansas, Texas, and The Dakotas. He created interesting pictorial records of frontier life and noted landscapes and anecdotes of adventurous pioneers. These images were creative and inspiring. In this scene, three cowboys are running away from American Indians. One of them has fallen off of his horse, and the others are trying to help him. Remington is a skillful artist. His colors are bright and his drawing is strong and effective.

Plate 8
John J. Audubon, *Washington Sea Eagle*, c. 1836-1839,
Smithsonian American Art Museum, Washington, D.C.

This renowned naturalist, ornithologist, and painter created fascinating paintings of North American wildlife. His paintings were often flat and polished, with incorrect details and false poses of the animals. In 1814, he spotted a strange, magnificent bird. It was a huge brown eagle with uncommon behavior. The creature was a fearless hunter and diver. He shot this mysterious raptor, examined it, and described it as a new species. Its dignity and toughness motivated him to name the bird Washington's Eagle, in honor of the first President of the United States. Biologists accepted this discovery, and this painting is Audubon's artistic representation of the bird. Scientists later concluded that Audubon had made a mistake, and rejected Washington's eagle as a recognizable species.